NETWORK MARKETING UNPLUGGED:

WHAT MY UPLINE NEVER TOLD ME

by
Odessa Hopkins

Network Marketing Unplugged: What My Upline Never Told Me

© Copyright 2013 Odessa Hopkins

ISBN: 978-0615825410

DEDICATION

This book is dedicated to my wonderful husband, Rick, for introducing me to the controversial, yet rewarding, network marketing industry. Being married to a workaholic is not easy, but you are second only to God! Thank you for loving me.

To my nieces, siblings and cousins: I seek always to make you proud. I am living proof that all things are possible when you work hard, have faith and believe in yourself. When in doubt, reach beyond the impossibilities to find the possibilities that God has waiting for only you.

CONTENTS

ACKNOWLEDGEMENTS

I'm thankful first, and always, to God for planting the seed in me to write this book.

Thanks to Spencer LaCapra, Keith Tucker and Marcella Rutherford for being the best network marketing leaders an associate could have. Your leadership, guidance, instruction and support have allowed me to grow my network marketing business, while not neglecting my primary business.

To Melanie Bonita, Author of Daily Dose of Determination, I send a daily dose of hugs and appreciation for staying on top of me, and giving me that last push needed to complete this project. You have been such a blessing to so many – helping one author after another reach #1 Amazon Best Seller status. Continue on your journey to bring out the exceptional best in everyone you touch.

Thanks to everyone in my downline for trusting and becoming business partners. I truly appreciate you! Stay the course and continue to soar.

Finally, without the input and support of the following people, this project would have been incomplete and one sided.

Anthony Davis

Arketha Reid

Barrett Matthews

Berna Dean

Brenda Harding

Brian Beane

Cameron Gamble

Chafica Miles

Charles Brown

Connie Page

Devin Paige

Gloria Harris

Ibtesam Muhammad

James Tadow King

Kia Coppedge

Marcella Rutherford

Melanie Bonita

Michael Marshall

Odessa Hopkins

Patricia Clover

Rick Hopkins

Shirley Dorsey

Spencer LaCapra

Steve Morring

Tiana Demsey

Tracy Green

Trevor Otts

Turiya Hodge

Vanessa Ellington

Wendell Parker

INTRODUCTION

LEGAL vs. ILLEGAL BUSINESS

Wikipedia defines Multi-level marketing (MLM) as a marketing strategy in which the sales force is compensated not only for sales they personally generate, but also for the sales of the other salespeople that they recruit. This recruited sales force is referred to as the participant's "downline", and can provide multiple levels of compensation.

"I would rather earn 1% of 100 people's efforts

than 100% of my own efforts"

- John Paul Getty (American Billionaire)

A Pyramid Scheme, on the other hand, is built on an illegal practice where overall compensation is based on recruiting, not on the delivery of legitimate products or services.

Although your upline could be anyone placed above you in a network marketing company, we will refer to only the upline placed directly above you (the person who personally introduced - or sponsored - you to the business).

Your upline was probably excited about telling you how to become a Millionaire in Network Marketing by selling tons of products and services or by recruiting an army of people. But there was likely something along the way they failed to tell you.

Let's face it, your upline did not join the business to be an educator and neither did you. You may have joined the business to generate income to support your lifestyle in your working years, or to continue that lifestyle in your retirement years. Whether one or both are true, learning certain details about the industry, in the early stages – such as the four compensation models – could be vital to your success or failure in network marketing.

I do hope that you did not join this industry to make fast cash because, as you may have already found out – a true network marketing company is not a "get rich quick" scheme. It's a business!

This book is designed to provide many aspects of the industry – from the four main payout models to how you can benefit from the industry without being a good salesman.

In order to provide a broad perspective, however, I have also included interviews with industry associates (both new, i.e. under one year in the industry and seasoned, i.e. over 15 years in the industry) who share the one thing their upline never told them.

This book is intended to help associates entering the business better understand the industry. It also serves as a tool to seasoned network marketing professionals of what their downline may want to know – but don't yet know how, or when, to ask.

This book, and the audio companion, makes a great gift for anyone entering, or currently in, the network marketing industry.

ONE

"Don is getting $10,000 a month in commission checks, and he just joined the business two months ago, so I know you can make $10,000 in commission in one."

Yes, indeed. Like me, many of you have heard this. What happens next is the adrenaline picks up; you get excited and envision all of your bills being paid off – in 90 days.

Well, something does actually happen in 90 days. You wake the heck up and realize that only you have been purchasing and consuming your own product.

What My Upline Never Told Me was that the people your upline described most likely left one company and went to another – convincing hundreds, or even thousands, of their downline to join them. Since they have the capability to bring a huge number of associates into the new business with them, the scenario makes sense – for them.

Keep in mind that unless the people who followed them also has a large downline, and was able to convince their downline to sign on to the move, they probably did not qualify for that car bonus or the $10,000 a month commission. However, your upline can't worry about that because they probably received a large cash incentive, from the new company, that came with certain stipulations.

That's right! Top leaders are often recruited by another company and paid thousands of dollars to jump. However, that sweet agreement often has one requirement: To convince a "large" portion of their downline to join them within a certain period of time. Otherwise, that money – you got it – must be returned. Ouch!

That's not to say that some people don't join a business, and hit bonuses, right out of the gate. Some people get right to work, focus on the prize and hit thousand dollar bonuses in their first few months – I'm one of them.

I hit enough $1,000 bonuses in my first few months to cover the monthly maintenance fee for the next two years. So, yes, it can be done! The point is not to join a business based on what someone else did. Your success, as with any business, is based – first – on your own effort. Learn the system, do the work, start building, and teach others to duplicate that.

According to the Direct Selling Association & U.S. Census statistics, by 2015, it is estimated that 50% of homes will be involved in the MLM Industry (U.S.).

Given those statistics, it's not whether network marketing is a serious industry. The question is, are you willing to ditch the fantasies and fallacies about making quick money

and put the time and energy into starting, growing and

running your business. Or, will you be one of the 97% that

fail?

TWO

"We have the best compensation plan in the industry!"

What My Upline Never Told Me is that every network marketing recruiter says the exact same thing. It's a sales business. Would any company admit to NOT having the best product, service or payout system? However, it could take months to even begin to unravel and comprehend the compensation plan of one company over another – especially if you're new to the industry. I was in three different companies before I met someone who explained to me not one, but the four main compensation plans used by most network marketing companies.

Your upline may show you a chart with lines, levels, people, generations, boxes, stats (with or without disclaimers); and, they may use terms like Binary, UniLevel, Breakaway or Forced Matrix.

The fact is, although each company's compensation plan is different, they are almost always based on one of the four main payout model structures.

Don't be lured by the cars, trips, bells and whistles unless it benefits YOU! If you need a new car, a company that offers a car program may be for you. If you love to travel, but can't find the money to travel as often as you would like, a travel bonus, or a travel company, may be perfect for you... Keep in mind that the bottom line should always be the cash compensation. Once you earn cash, you can buy your own car and pay for your own vacation. A perfect scenario is to find a company that offers the best of both worlds – great commission with cash, car and vacation bonuses. Good luck with that!

In order to benefit from any compensation plan, you must understand it and map out a plan of action, just as you would in your own, traditional business. Remember, this IS your independent business. Otherwise, you will miss your mark, place people incorrectly or get frustrated and claim the business did not work.

Prior to understanding the compensation plan of one business, I placed people in the wrong position and it cost me a pretty penny. Although I still made money, not educating myself on one simple rule prevented me from tripling my cash compensation.

In another business, a placement mistake almost cost me a $1000 bonus. Fortunately, the company was forgiving of those in the business less than 30 days, and I collected my bonus – hence one reason that company is still part of my business portfolio.

Before I consider an opportunity, I focus on six main areas: Products/services (2) Compensation (3) Time in Business

(4) Leadership (5) Training (6) Business Fees (startup/maintenance) – In no particular order!

THREE

Compensation Payout Models

Below are images, and descriptions, of the compensation payout models with a description of each plan in more detail. Each has pros and cons and should be carefully thought out prior to joining a business – or placing people into a business.

Note: *Spelling is intentionally kept original to the Network Marketing Business School author's European origin.*

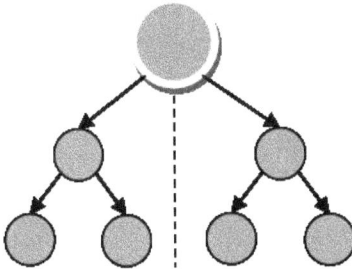

Binary

The Binary Plan as the name suggests is based around the number 2, which represents the maximum number of frontline associates that any business centre can have. Any additional distributors must then be placed under one of your existing frontline members. This creates a very supportive environment for new members as the easiest way for associates to achieve success is by assisting their new members to build their organisations. This team approach makes the binary plan very attractive as there is a lot of support (both initial and ongoing) as all associates within your organisation work towards achieving a common goal.

The main earning objective of the binary compensation plan is to balance the amount of leg volume flowing through either side of your business centre. For example if you had 800 sales points flowing through the left leg of your business but only 500 points flowing through the right, you are paid out on the highest common denominator which in this instance is 500 points. When the Binary Plan was first introduced any additional volume (ie the extra 300 points on the left) would be lost making it difficult for part timers however more recently most binary plans now allow any additional volume to be carried over to the following commission period. This carry over feature has proven to be very popular for part-timers as it means that you don't ever lose any of the sales volume that you have acquired.

Because the goal is to balance the volume flowing through your organization this encourages associates to help their weaker downline members to build their organization (promoting teamwork) to achieve a better volume balance and a more consistent (and higher) commission cheque.

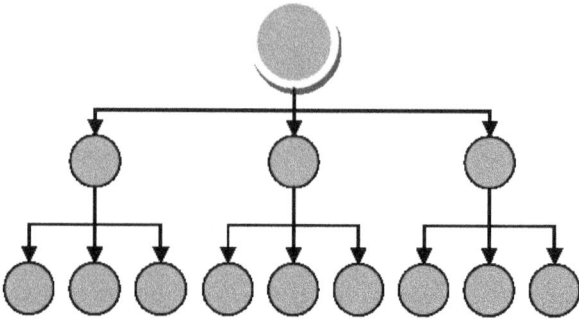

Forced Matrix

The Matrix Plan, also known as a Forced Matrix Plan, is based around a compensation structure that has a set width and depth for which distributors are compensated. Although there are many variations to this compensation plan, the basic concept remains the same.

The basic structure of this compensation plan is normally identified by a simple equation that distinguishes the width and depth of the plan (i.e. width x depth). For example a 3 x 5 plan suggests you can only sponsor a maximum of 3 frontline distributors and you have the potential to earn commissions up to 5 levels deep.

Because there is a limited width to this compensation structure, distributors are encouraged to assist their downline members to help their organisation grow. Additionally any new recruits that are sponsored after your frontline is full must be positioned under one of your existing downline distributors. This process is commonly referred to as spill over which is also used in the Binary Plan. The main advantage of this concept is that it creates an element of team work where some distributors within your organisation can work together and mutually benefit.

The Forced Matrix structure allows distributors to sponsor new recruits deeper into their downline once their frontline is full. Traditionally these new distributors were automatically placed into the next available position;

however, more recently, plans have been developed to allow distributors to decide where they want to position these new distributors. This recent modification has made this structure more appealing, as it gives distributors more control over their business and it increases the amount of teamwork.

One of the main advantages of the Matrix Plan over the Unilevel Plan and Stairstep Breakaway is once your frontline is full, your focus now changes towards developing your frontline distributors and assisting them to find and train their frontline distributors and so on.

A potential setback of the Matrix Plan is that generally the amount of commissions paid on each level is variable. Therefore there is more incentive for distributors to assist some levels of their downline but not others. Additionally, some plans are quite wide and may require you to fill 6 or more frontline positions before assisting your frontline to develop their organisation. Another drawback to the variable commission rate is while it does offer some incentives it can be hard to explain to potential prospects. You could have the best company in the world but if the compensation plan is too hard to explain or understand it can make it very difficult to convert potential prospects.

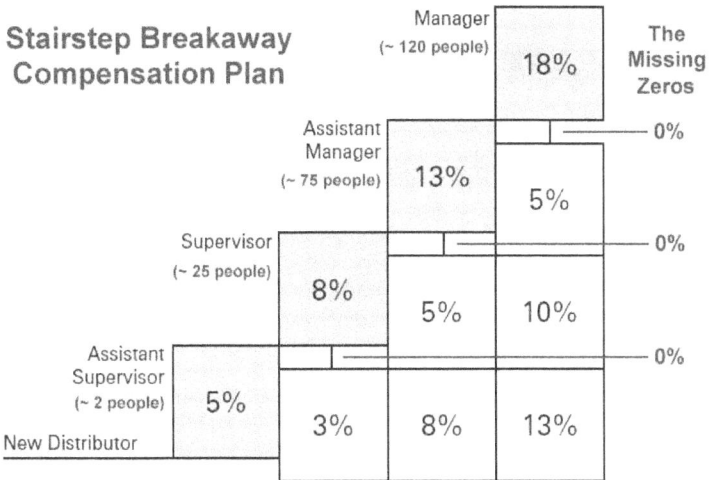

Stairstep Breakaway

The Stair Step Breakaway Plan was one of the original network marketing compensation plans and is still used by a number of foundation companies today. Given that this structure has been around for many years and has a proven track record it is still commonly implemented by new start up companies, however, just like all compensation structures whilst there are some advantages to this compensation structure, there are also a number of disadvantages which will be discussed on this page.

The name Stair Step Breakaway is derived from the concept that distributors climb the ladder of success and when they reach a certain level they are allowed to break away from their upline distributors and run their organisation independently. As distributors break away from their upline this allows them to earn a greater commission. The Stair Step Breakaway Plan shares a number of similarities with Unilevel Plan in that each distributor is only allowed to sponsor one level of distributors (frontline). Whilst there is no limit to the width (number of frontline distributors) in which you can sponsor, the stair step breakaway plan offers limited incentive for teamwork within your organisation and the competition between crossline distributors can make it difficult to recruit close friends and family into this structure.

As with all network marketing companies, the main goal for each business associate is to distribute the parent company's products. This is best achieved in the stair step break away plan by recruiting as many frontline distributors as you can, who personally consume and /or sell your company's product and then encourage them to do the same.

The Breakaway

Breaking away from your upline has numerous benefits to the individual distributor (such as earning a higher commission rate), however it can have a serious negative impact to the organisation in which you break away from. By breaking away, the volume that your upline previously received from you, no longer flows through your upline's business at the same rate. For your upline, it is like losing their best customers.

As distributors breakaway, the original sponsor is still entitled to earn a small percentage from each break away distributors's efforts. This is referred to as an ***override commission***. Each breakaway organisation is referred to as a ***generation*** and although distributors are entitled to earn an override commission on all of their breakaway generations, unfortunately this override commission is only a small fraction in comparison to the commissions they were earning previously.

Another setback with the Stair Step Breakaway Plan is that although you may have reached the level where you are allowed to break away from you upline, allowing you to earn greater commission, your organisation will grow and distributors in your downline may also qualify to break away from you. Although initially having a distributor break away from your organisation can put a dent in your short-term income, creating a number of breakaway organisations can help you to earn a long term residual income and re-focus your time towards developing a frontline of future leaders.

In general, this plan is most suited to those distributors who are confident in their ability to recruit new distributors and have good management skills. For those looking at this compensation plan for the first time, one thing to consider

is that you may experience a lack of support from your

upline distributors once you are established and that you

will be working in competition with other crossline

distributors. Whilst the potential commissions can be very

rewarding with this compensation structure, the Binary

Plan and the Matrix Plan are generally considered more

friendly and supportive for newcomers.

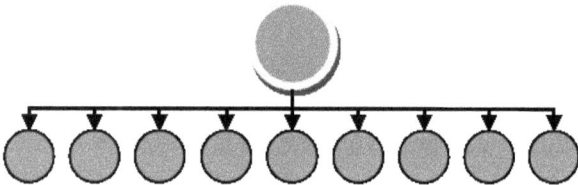

Unilevel

The Unilevel plan has been around for many years and

given its proven track record it is still used by a number of

network marketing companies today. The main benefit to

this model is that is very easy to understand, however like all compensation plans, whilst there are some benefits there are also a number of setbacks that should also be considered.

Unilevel, as the name suggests, only enables you to sponsor one line of distributors, therefore everyone you sponsor is on your frontline. There are no width limitations to this plan (ie there is no limit to the amount of people you can sponsor in your frontline) and commissions are normally paid out on a limited depth (common plans that we have reviewed pay commissions between 5 and 7 levels deep). Therefore, the common goal of this plan is to recruit a large number of frontline distributors and then encourage them to do the same.

To earn a commission using this structure there is normally only a minimal amount of personal volume that is required, which essentially makes it easier for part-timers to earn an income. Although it tends to be easier to earn a commission using this compensation structure, when comparing it to other plans, the structure itself restricts the total amount of each commission you can earn (i.e. although it is easier to earn commissions you do not tend to earn as much).

One of the main disadvantages of the plan is that every distributor you sponsor becomes crossline to all of your other frontline distributors and therefore must work in competition with the others. This can present numerous challenges for the newcomer who attempts to recruit friends and family into their business, as in essence, they will be working in competition to one another. An ever increasing frontline also requires continual training and having to manage large numbers of people.

The unilevel plan does, however, have a few advantages, mainly the fact that it is easy to explain. Generally, the more distributors you recruit, the greater your commission cheque. This makes it attractive to your experienced network marketers, particularly those that are gun recruiters (top-of-the-line seasoned leaders) and have the ability to develop management and training systems for their growing downline.

Given the competition created between frontline distributors within this compensation structure, it is common practice for distributors within this plan to target their cold market (people they don't know) as a way to build their organisation. This may include developing lead generation systems and the use of internet leads.

NOTE: *Compensation models are compliments of the Network Marketing School of Business.*

Hybrid Compensation Plan

Sometimes companies will combine one or more plans to create their own compensation model.

FOUR

"You don't have to do any work. Just join the business and I will do the rest."

What My Upline Never Told Me was that while they will hit their quota when I come in the business, once they do, I will go to the bottom of their priority list. No one should enter into any business with the expectation of getting paid for doing nothing. If that were true, it would not be called a "business" opportunity, would it?

As with any business, network marketing is about the numbers. If you don't hit the numbers, you will not be compensated. Each individual is in the business to make "their" numbers and to teach you to do the same. It's called "duplication." That is not to say your upline will not be supportive or responsive. It means you are responsible for attending meetings and trainings to learn the business and to become successful in "your" business. Check with people in the business prior to joining to get a feel for the leadership. You can usually assess how much support you will, or will not, get based on the leadership. Hands-off leaders often produce a hands-off downline because that is what they have duplicated.

FIVE

"You will make lots of money selling this product.

Everyone needs it."

What My Upline Never Told Me was that people buy things

they want – not things they need. They buy on emotion.

Good business people – particularly sales people know this.

Yet, your sales script (or pitch) is not something they

typically teach you to work on after recruiting you, and not

all back offices are equipped with the necessary documents

and tools to help make their associates (or distributors)

successful. Be sure to check the company's back office to

see what you will be getting with your signup fee. Most

businesses come with a startup and maintenance fee.

Check to see whether the startup fee includes a replicated

website (included with any reputable network marketing

business). Also, check the back office for – at the very

least – a business presentation (slides and/or video), sales scripts, product videos, sales reports and up-to-date compensation package (slides and/or video). Even if you are a seasoned network marketing expert, and have no use for some of these items – such as a sales script – most of the people you recruit will.

SIX

"When you come into the business, introduce the product to your family and friends. They will support you."

What My Upline Never Told Me was that family members are often the least likely candidates to support you in any business – and network marketing is no exception.

In fact, it's less likely they will support you in this industry if they have already pre-determined, from what someone has told them, that it is "one of those things" – meaning a pyramid scheme. They have probably not taken the time to educate themselves on the difference between a pyramid scheme and a legal network marketing business. It's unlikely they would do so now. It certainly does not hurt to approach them and, if your family supports you in other ventures, they will likely support you in this one. Just don't bet on it and, by all means, do not get disappointed.

Also, always invite someone who turned down the opportunity to become a customer – especially supportive friends and family members. Remember, not everyone is interested in being an entrepreneur, but everyone is a customer of something.

In addition to the last four compensation models, there is the Hybrid model, which could be any combination of the main four.

SEVEN

"The number one advantage you will have in this business is the money you will quickly earn."

What My Upline Never Told Me was that the first advantage of entering into business, particularly while working a traditional job, are the tax benefits. By simply updating your allowances, you could add an additional $100 to $400 dollars to your "current" paycheck. The government offers business owners who work as little as four or five hours a week on their business (which is considered full-time) over 300 tax deductions. The IRS has stated that 80% of taxpayers overpay their taxes – 80%!

Here's the best part. Although you are in business to generate revenue, you are eligible for these deductions whether, or not, you do so. Check the IRS website, and speak with your accountant, to learn more about tax advantages for business owners. Remember, as a network marketing independent representative, you ARE a business owner! I will repeat that throughout this book because it's the one thing network marketing affiliates (or associates) seem not to understand.

Another item I will bundle in this section, that My Upline Never Told Me was the importance of tracking expenses (as a business owner). Now, I must be honest. I was already in business, so I knew how important expense tracking is, but I knew if my upline did not tell me, it's likely they did not tell others either.

Many people do not join a networking marketing opportunity thinking of it as a "real" business. They think of it as just something they're doing to make a few extra dollars – or some join with hopes of becoming a millionaire – different strokes for different people. So, they leave weeks or months later after failing to realize their first level of benefits – tax deductions.

As with any business, expenses and income must be tracked in order to receive the tax. My husband and I, both business owners (traditional and network marketing), use a simple system called the CashFlow Manager (www.trackcashflow.com). It's a simple system we use to track expenses, mileage and travel from our phone. It also has a receipt capture feature built in – which is especially great if you get audited. There are others on the market as well, so feel free to research. Whichever one you choose, just start tracking your business mileage (including those weekly opportunity meetings and trips to see prospects), your restaurant and travel expenses, your home office and utilities (including phone, electric, Internet…), medical expenses, car loan and maintenance… There are tons of deductions, but you MUST track them to qualify for the deduction – so make it part of the process towards your financial success plan.

EIGHT

"Start this business to leave a legacy for your spouse, children or grandchildren."

What My Upline Never Told Me was that not all network marketing businesses allow you to transfer, or sell, your position in the business. In fact, most don't. Check with the company "before" you start building your downline to make sure you're building something you can leave as a legacy or sell back to the company for monetary compensation towards your retirement.

Of course, the best way to leave a legacy is to save and invest a percentage of your commission, while you are building your business. That way, it is not based on whether or not you can transfer, or sell, your business in a particular company.

NINE

"If you have a lot of friends, you will do great."

What My Upline Never Told Me was that "I would have to separate myself from my old friends and surround myself with new ones." This one was actually a Brian Beane original taken from the audio companion of this book.

The truth is, like family, your friends are sometimes critical, or jealous, of your success. So, they may be less likely to support you than you might imagine. That's not to say you will not have very supportive family and friends. It's to say, be prepared if Brian's experience is yours.

Brian Bean is an International Coach and Founder of Mentor to Millions.

TEN

"This company has a Mercedes program. Build your team and they will give you a free car."

What My Upline Never Told Me me is that they know more people who "had" the car than those who still "have" the car. That's often because many car programs are based on (1) Qualifying for the car and (2) Staying Qualified for the car. Once your product sales or new recruit numbers drop below a certain number, the car is swooped up by either the network marketing company or the leasing company – depending on the program. If the company is leasing the car for you, it has been repossessed. Or, if you leased the car yourself, chances are, you are in jeopardy of destroying your credit for turning the car in before your lease is up. Let's face it, if you could have afforded a

Mercedes, you probably would have leased or bought one prior to joining the business.

Most car programs are great. Just don't lease your ego, instead of the car. When you lease your ego, you don't take into account the criteria of keeping, or losing, it. A friend of mine qualified for the car within her first two months of joining her first network marketing business. She opted not to take the car, and decided to continue building her business and sacking away the cash commissions. That decision turned out to be the right one – for her.

With six months in that business, the leadership fell apart, meeting locations were non-existent, the company was not keeping up with technology and the commission checks stopped coming. Had she taken the car, it would have been repossessed six months later. Instead, she is enjoying the investment she made by tucking away her commission

checks.

ELEVEN

"If you don't like the company's system,

create your own."

This was, by far, the worst advice I received – and followed! One of the key rules of network marketing is to utilize and duplicate the system the company put in place. The key here is to duplicate. A good network marketing company will invest a lot of planning, thought, time and money to create a system that their associates can duplicate. If you join a business and, immediately, start recreating it – especially prior to learning the business and current system, you are setting yourself, and your downline, up to FAIL! If you want to create your own system, create your own company. The beauty of network marketing is that the system is already there for you. The money and thought has already been put into it. Sure, adjust the script to where it has your personalized feel and touch, because people buy people, but don't recreate the system. And, by all means, don't teach your downline to recreate it either. Their hands will be full just trying to master the exciting system.

When I began writing this book, I felt it was important to share things my upline never told "me." But, after more careful thought, I realized people needed to hear more than just my perspective. Just as you can learn from my experience, you could learn much more from what others have learned as well.

Below is the text version of 30 interviews I did with network marketing professionals. NO companies were mentioned. The purpose of the interviews was not to criticize the business, associate or the industry.

The truth is, if you have recruited even one person into a network marketing business, it is simply impossible to tell them everything they need to know about the industry.

Much of what they will learn will be in the meetings,

training sessions and, like me, through experience along the

way. Nevertheless, this book, and audio companion, will

take some of the guess work out so they can enjoy the

journey.

TWELVE

You Are Not Alone:

Below are responses from 30 network marketing professionals I interviewed for this book. When asked, "What's one thing your upline never told you?", these were their responses. Some of the responses were followed up with an brief explanation on the audio.

Some of the responses may be questions to ask your upline, and some may be irrelevant to you. Just remember that the associates interviewed have been in the industry between six months to 30 years, so most, although not all, of the questions are very relative to your success.

My upline never told me...

> How to utilize my cashflow system by plugging in my information and writing off my taxes.

- I must constantly talk to people about what I do.

- It's not about what works. It's about what's duplicatable.

- I would be hooked, because I would love it so much.

- How much work it would take to start up.

- Information about the tax advantages vs. selling the products.

- How to be very successful in the industry.

- I must have different types of systems for each part of my business.

- Most people will earn more money from tax savings than product sales in the first few years in the business.

- It would be hard to find somebody that understood what it takes to be in network marketing.

- You have to find people who sell the product, from the heart, and not just the dream.
- That there are so many different payout models, and how to maximize them.
- How much they really make in network marketing.
- The numbers are the numbers. You must really go through a lot of people to find true leaders.
- How simple it is to sponsor or bring people into the business if you relax and act like you are talking to your best friend.
- How rewarding and fulfilling it would be.
- It would be lots of hard work, but you would take care of a lot of people in the process.
- I should use my personality to do the presentation. Because I love people and people love my personality, it would have made a big difference.

- People are very skeptical about doing business in the network marketing industry, at first, because they don't understand it.
- The fortune is in the follow up. Most people are not going to call you about the opportunity. You have to call them.
- I would have to invest money in my business, to build my business, if I want a large business.
- I would have to communicate with people all the time.
- How important it was to separate myself from my old friends and surround myself with new ones.
- When you are trying to market your business, you have to market yourself more than your business because people join people, not businesses.
- How to make money with money.

- The first year is a building period. I may or may not do well but, if I can hang in there, I would do better the second year.
- What to do when you run out of family and friends.
- What the reason is behind networking. How to network and be successful at it.
- To put money away while you are building the business to have a cushion should the business end.

This book comes with an audio CD companion which includes responses of all 30 interviews. In it, you will hear some of the expanded responses directly from people who have been in the industry for more than 20 years.

To Request the Audio Companion via Inbox and/or CD:
Email your name, address and the date and place of purchase to cd@networkmarketingunplugged.com. The

audio file will be delivered to your inbox upon receipt. A copy of the CD will be mailed to the address provided (U.S. only) within 24 hours of receipt. Please put: "Audio Companion" in the subject line of your email (required).

Everything about the network marketing industry will not be found in either this book, or on the CD, since much of what is learned is done so over the life of your network marketing career. However, this set will help you better understand the industry, and provide nuggets as well as questions to ask your upline before getting too deep into the business.

Purchase the book and audio companion for yourself, your downline, upline or anyone interested in the network marketing industry so they can no longer say, "My Upline Never Told Me."

48

www.ingramcontent.com/pod-product-compliance
Lightning Source LLC
Chambersburg PA
CBHW050521210326
41520CB00012B/2395